W9-CMS-440

WAYNE PUBLIC LIBRARY
~~PREAKNESS BRANCH~~
~~1006 HAMBURG TURNPIKE~~
WAYNE, NJ 07470

OCT 2 6 2016

WAYNE PUBLIC LIBRARY
PREAKNESS BRANCH
1006 HAMBURG TURNPIKE
WAYNE, NJ 07470

KNITTING PATTERNS TO WARM THE SOUL

WITHIN

In Memory of
Karen Stiner
Kaplysz

JANE RICHMOND & SHANNON COOK

MARIAN RAE PUBLICATIONS

OCT 2 6 2016

ACCEPT WHAT IS,
LET GO OF WHAT WAS,
AND BELIEVE IN WHAT WILL BE.
BE YOU.

Copyright © 2016 Marian Rae Publications

All rights reserved. No portion of this publication
may be reproduced, stored in a retrieval system, or
transmitted in any form or by any means, mechanical,
electronic, photocopying, recording, or otherwise,
without written permission from the publisher.
For personal use only.

MARIAN RAE PUBLICATIONS
Artistic & inspiring books for the modern knitter.

Published in Canada by Marian Rae Publications.
www.marianraepublications.com

ISBN 978-0-9917289-2-3

Cover & book design by Shannon Cook
Editing by Austen Gilliland
Technical editing by Anne Marie Hart
Copy editing by Jessie Kwak
Proofreading by Lisa Fielding
Modelling by Gryffin Hoskins & Mark Spencer
Photography by KGOODPHOTO (Pages 1–77,
122–126, 128–131, cover)
Photography by Shannon Cook (Pages 78–114, 127)
Illustrations by Shannon Cook (Pages 85, 95)
Illustrations by Jane Richmond (Pages 117, 120–121)
Styling by Shannon Cook & Jane Richmond

First Edition
Printed in China

78

86

96

100

104

108

TABLE OF CONTENTS

JANE

I always find it difficult to write introductions – we have spent the better part of a year putting everything together. Patterns envisioned, written, rewritten, edited, tested, reconsidered, and reviewed. Pages have been pored over for months; photos scrutinized pixel by pixel, and carefully placed into the final layout. At this point, Shannon and I have spent so much time looking at these pages, it's now hard to step back and see what the final book has become.

Recently, my friend Cate asked me to describe the theme of this book. This collection is inspired by winter. It's true, winter can be harsh and blustery, but we knitters secretly revel in the opportunity to wrap ourselves in wool. We create our warmest and coziest projects in deep winter: cozy woollens you might bring camping or to a cabin in the woods, to be worn around the fire or tromping through the snow. Well-made, reliable knitwear for every day, the kind you throw on first thing to ward off the chill of a frosty morning.

At the heart of this vision of warmth is our model, Gryffin. She's strong, independent, and enjoys the quiet of a solo adventure. We envisioned her surrounded by the harsh cold of winter, sitting by the fire, alone with her thoughts, warm in her handknits and fulfilled by her own inner peace. She has followed her own path here and has done it her own way, and she is happy with where it has led her.

With our vision clear, our insightful photographer planted a seed. What about a new person in this story...had we considered a boyfriend? We trusted the brilliant instincts and vision of our photographer, Kelsey, and our solo girl was now partnered up with a handsome and worthy boyfriend.

I was struck by how Gryffin is both strong and autonomous when alone and when part of a couple. She is capable, contented, and independently happy. As a result, she is able to be there, with him, engaged and completely present, yet still an individual, who is true to herself. The progression of her story, and the shift it has created, is beautiful. A clear message unfolds, about finding true happiness outside of ourselves only after we've found it within.

As I finished telling Cate about the theme of this book, I knew that I wanted to share it with you as well. I hope you find what you need in this collection – warmth, inspiration, strength, ruggedness, solitude, and, of course, well-made winter knits.

SHANNON

"Quiet the mind, and the soul will speak...."

Oh, how those words speak directly to my heart. Since Jane and I released *Seasonless* in 2014, I have found myself searching for insight into my true identity. This path has had many twists and turns as I search for personal growth and change. Every time I think I've reached my destination, the path swiftly changes directions and keeps me longing for more. My journey keeps me awake at night and energized throughout the day. It keeps me at peace but also stirs my mind.

For me, creativity has always been as important as breathing. It's a part of my soul and what makes me, me. Without it, I would feel lost. Without it, I wouldn't be me. I strongly believe that we should all spend at least a few minutes each day nurturing our creative side. But sometimes life can get in the way, and we begin to feel unbalanced. When my balance shifted, I knew I needed to make some big changes in my life to allow myself to continue on a healthy, creative journey.

This imbalance led me to finding and embracing mindfulness and meditation. They have become a welcome addition to my everyday life as a mother, wife, and friend, and in my creative life and business. When we began working on *Within,* I was just beginning to learn how to take back control of my overall health. These projects were all designed during this time, and each one holds a special memory of my path to self-discovery. Each piece is rhythmic and relaxing to knit, yet never boring. Each pattern is a gentle path to follow while you knit. The garments and accessories are comforting and cozy – the type of pieces you want to curl up in each day.

"Knowing yourself is the beginning of all wisdom."

Learning to accept and feel comfortable with yourself can sometimes be a scary and tricky thing. But once you face that fear head-on and make friends with it, learning about and accepting your true self becomes much easier. The ability to feel comfortable, happy, and at peace with yourself can truly allow you to embrace your life with others.

When we strip away all the outside distractions that life throws our way, we are left with our inner selves. So embrace who you are, relish in your creative mind, strive for balance, and cultivate and nurture your soul. You are good enough. You are worth the few precious moments a day you can take to indulge in your personal creativity. Take care of yourself.

I hope you enjoy our newest collection and find happiness in those precious moments you find in your day to bask in the joy of handmade.

HERE'S TO

Winter

TO COZY CABINS

AND LANTERN LIGHT,

TO SETTLING IN TO

THE SCENT OF FRESHLY

CUT WOOD AND

HEAVENLY CANDLES,

AND TO MOMENTS SHARED

BESIDE THE WARMTH

OF A ROARING FIRE.

HUDSON

Early morning:
Sunlight filters in,
and mist rises
from the fields.

Wrap yourself in
warmth; go forth to
greet the dawn.

PAGE / 86

TIMBER

*Shrug on another
layer and prepare to
meet the day.*

*What secrets do the
coming hours hold?*

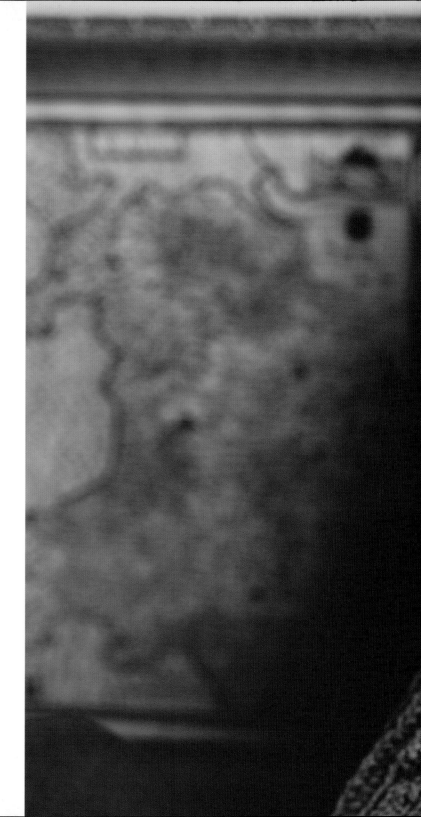

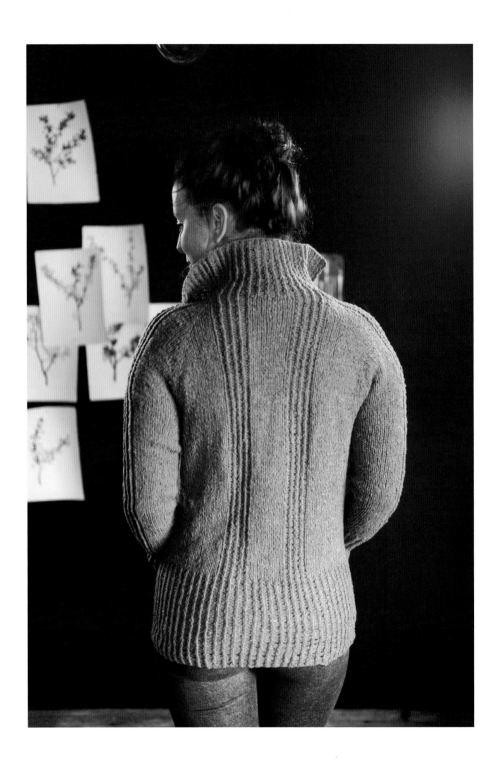

ENTWINE

Luxurious layers encircle you in a woolly embrace.

The golden hour approaches.

PAGE / 100

TREAD

*Another day is
nearly done.*

*Trap the heat of
the sun's last rays
in a luscious,
textured knit.*

WOODSTACK

*Warm hands, warm
heart – campfire not
entirely optional.*

PAGE / 108

FIRESIDE

Darkness has fallen;
evening has arrived.

Settle in to the
night's embrace.

Patterns

HUDSON SHAWL

by SHANNON COOK

This shawl is a relaxing project that features addictive stripes paired with textured openwork, with a pretty edging that adds a bit of knitterly interest. Hudson is a quick knit that's so much fun to make, you won't want to put it down. The finished product is a generously sized accessory that can be styled many ways. It's a shawl that just begs to be wrapped up in – no matter the season.

YARN

Cascade Yarns Ecological Wool (100% Undyed Peruvian Highland Wool, 478yds/437m per 8.75oz/250g skein), bulky

1 skein in MC, shown in Beige (8016) OR approx 371yds/330m, 194g of bulky (or heavy chunky) weight yarn

Cascade Yarns Eco + (100% Peruvian Highland Wool, 478yds/437m per 8.75oz/250g skein), bulky

1 skein in CC #1, shown in Straw (4010) OR approx 58yds/52m, 30g of bulky (or heavy chunky) weight yarn

1 skein in CC #2, shown in Yakima Heather (9459) OR approx 182yds/166m, 95g of bulky (or heavy chunky) weight yarn

1 skein in CC #3, shown in Pumpkin Spice (2453) OR approx 29yds/26m, 15g of bulky (or heavy chunky) weight yarn

GAUGE

13 sts and 20 rows = 4in/10cm in St st, blocked

NEEDLES

6mm/US 10 – long circular needle recommended

Adjust needle size if necessary to obtain proper gauge.

NOTIONS

Stitch markers – 4
Removable stitch marker

FINISHED MEASUREMENTS

Approx 70in/178cm wingspan and 35in/89cm depth, blocked

STITCH GUIDE

m1 (EZ's Backwards Loop Version): With stitches on your right needle, wrap working yarn around your left index finger from back to front. Insert tip of right needle under front of loop on finger. Remove finger and pull yarn gently to snug loop around needle. On next row, treat the loop as a separate stitch. Take care to pull the stitch nice and tight so it blends in.

m1L (make one left): With left needle tip, lift strand between needles from front to back. Knit lifted loop through the back. This will make a left-slanting increase.

m1R (make one right): With left needle tip, lift strand between needles from back to front. Knit lifted loop through the front. This will make a right-slanting increase.

Openwork Stitch:
Row 1 (RS): Knit.
Row 2: Purl.
Rows 3, 4 & 6: Knit.
Row 5: *K2tog, yo; rep from * to end.

PATTERN NOTES

You will be increasing 4 stitches on every **RS** row. Slip all markers as you come to them throughout the pattern. A **Pattern Stitch Count Chart** is shown on **Page 85**.

When working the 2-row colour changes of the **Main Shawl**, simply carry the strand you've just finished up the side along with the new working strand. For sections longer than 2 rows, we recommend cutting your yarn and tying in the new colour. Your ends will be woven in after blocking.

While working the **Knit-On Edging**, on every **RS** row you will be using 1 stitch from your new cast-on stitches and 1 stitch from your existing stitches for the k2tog at the end of the row. This will bind-off 1 existing stitch each **RS** row. Remove all stitch markers as you come to them while working the **Knit-On Edging**.

SET UP

Using the **Long Tail Cast-On** and CC #1, CO 3 sts (*see* **Special Techniques** *on* **Page 120** *for link to visual tutorial*).

You may choose to work your "m1" increases throughout with **EZ's Backwards Loop Version** or with **m1R** (before the stitch marker) and **m1L** (after the stitch marker), depending on your personal preference. Both versions are explained in the **Stitch Guide** on **Page 79**.

Row 1 (RS): [K1, m1] twice, k1. Place removable marker on this side to denote **RS**. (5 sts)

Rows 2, 4 & 6 (WS): Knit.

Rows 3 & 5: [K1, m1] to last st, k1. (17 sts)

Row 7: [K5, pm, m1, k1, m1, pm] twice, k5. (21 sts)

Rows 8 & 10: [K5, sm, p to m, sm] twice, k5.

Row 9: [K5, sm, m1, k to m, m1, sm] twice, k5. (25 sts)

MAIN SHAWL – STRIPES

STRIPE PATTERN SET-UP

Change to MC.

Row 11 (RS): [K5, sm, m1, k to m, m1, sm] twice, k5. (29 sts)

Row 12: [K5, sm, p to m, sm] twice, k5.

Change to Colour CC #1.

Rows 13 & 14: Rep **Rows 11 & 12**. (33 sts)

Change to MC.

Rows 15 & 16: Rep **Rows 11 & 12**. (37 sts)

Change to CC #1.

Rows 17 & 18: Rep **Rows 11 & 12**. (41 sts)

Change to MC.

Rows 19–22: Rep **Rows 11 & 12** twice. (49 sts)

MAIN STRIPE PATTERN – CC #2

Continue in MC.

Rows 23 & 24: Rep **Rows 11 & 12**. (53 sts)

Change to CC #2.

Rows 25 & 26: Rep **Rows 11 & 12**. (57 sts)

Change to MC.

Rows 27 & 28: Rep **Rows 11 & 12**. (61 sts)

Change to CC #2.

Rows 29 & 30: Rep **Rows 11 & 12**. (65 sts)

Change to MC.

Rows 31 & 32: Rep **Rows 11 & 12**. (69 sts)

Change to CC #2.

Rows 33–38: Rep **Rows 11 & 12** three times. (81 sts)

MAIN STRIPE PATTERN – CC #3

Change to MC.

Rows 39–54: Rep **Rows 23–38** using MC and CC #3 (in place of CC #2). (113 sts)

MAIN STRIPE PATTERN – CC #1

Change to MC.

Rows 55–70: Rep **Rows 23–38** using MC and CC #1 (in place of CC #2). (145 sts)

MAIN SHAWL – OPENWORK

Change to MC.

Row 71: [K5, sm, m1, k to m, m1, sm] twice, k5. (149 sts)

Row 72: [K5, sm, p to m, sm] twice, k5.

Row 73: Rep **Row 71**. (153 sts)

Rows 74 & 76: Knit.

Row 75: K5, sm, m1, [k2tog, yo] to last st before m, k1, m1, sm, k5, sm, m1, k1, [yo, k2tog] to m, m1, sm, k5. (157 sts)

Rows 77–112: Rep **Rows 71–76** six times. (229 sts)

Rows 113 & 114: Rep **Rows 71 & 72**. (233 sts)

MAIN SHAWL – GARTER STITCH

Rows 115 & 117: [K5, sm, m1, k to m, m1, sm] twice, k5. (241 sts)

Rows 116 & 118: Knit.

Change to CC #3.

Rows 119 & 120: Rep **Rows 115 & 116**. (245 sts)

Change to MC.

Rows 121 & 122: Rep **Rows 115 & 116**. (249 sts)

Change to CC #2.

Rows 123 & 124: Rep **Rows 115 & 116**. (253 sts)

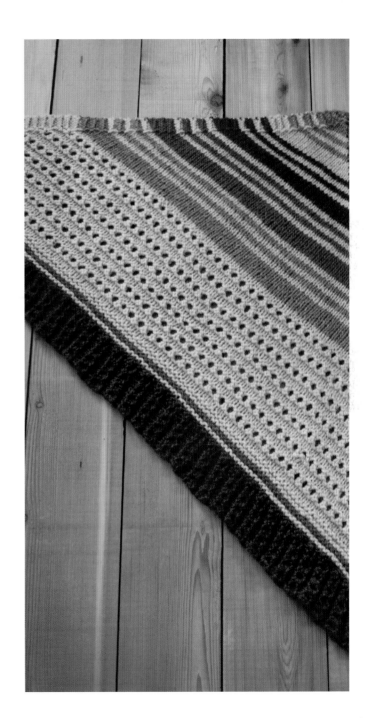

KNIT·ON EDGING

Remove markers as you come to them. You will be turning your work after each row unless otherwise instructed.

Continuing with CC #2 and **RS** facing you, use the **Cable Cast-On Method** to CO 9 sts (*see* **Stitch Guide** *on* **Page 118** *for link to visual tutorial*).

Do not turn your work (*you will begin turning your work AFTER you complete* **Row 1** *below*).

GARTER STITCH (SECTION 1)

Row 1 (RS): K8, k2tog (this will be 1 st from your newly CO sts and 1 st from your existing border.) Turn work. 1 st dec'd.

Row 2: K9. Turn work.

Row 3: K8, k2tog. Turn work. 1 st dec'd.

Rows 4–9: Rep **Rows 2 & 3** of this section three times.

Shawl will now have 248 shawl sts and 9 edge sts.

Row 10: Rep **Row 2** of this section.

OPENWORK (SECTION 1)

Continue turning your work after each row as established.

Rows 1 & 3 (RS): K8, k2tog. 1 st dec'd.

Row 2: P9.

Rows 4 & 6: K9.

Row 5: [K2tog, yo] four times, k2tog. 1 st dec'd.

Shawl will now have 245 shawl sts and 9 edge sts.

Rep **Rows 1–6** of this section, thirty-eight times more, ending 2 sts before next marker.

Shawl will now have 131 shawl sts and 9 edge sts.

Next Row: K8, k3tog. 2 sts dec'd.

Next Row: P9.

Shawl will now have 129 shawl sts and 9 edge sts.

SHORT ROW SECTION

Continue turning your work after each row unless otherwise instructed.

Row 1 (RS): K8, k2tog. 1 st dec'd.

Rows 2, 6, 8, 10 & 14: K9.

Row 3 (RS): K8, sl 1 st from LH needle to RH needle purl-wise. Bring yarn from back of work to front. Sl st back from RH needle to LH needle. Turn work. Your yarn will now be in back of work.

Row 4: K8.

Rows 5, 9 & 13: K8, k2tog. 1 st dec'd.

Row 7 (Centre Stitch of Shawl): K8, k2tog. 1 st dec'd.

Row 11: Rep **Row 3** of this section.

Row 12: K8.

Shawl will now have 124 shawl sts and 9 edge sts.

OPENWORK (SECTION 2)

Continue turning your work after each row as established.

Row 1 (RS): K8, k3tog. 2 sts dec'd.

Row 2: P9.

Row 3: K8, k2tog. 1 st dec'd.

Rows 4 & 6: K9.

Row 5: [K2tog, yo] four times, k2tog. 1 st dec'd.

Rows 7 & 9: K8, k2tog. 1 st dec'd.

Row 8: P9.

Rows 10 & 12: K9.

Row 11: [K2tog, yo] four times, k2tog. 1 st dec'd.

Shawl will now have 117 shawl sts and 9 edge sts.

Rep **Rows 7–12** of this section, thirty-seven times more, ending 1 st before next marker.

Shawl will now have 6 shawl sts and 9 edge sts.

Next Row: K8, k2tog. 1 st dec'd.

Next Row: P9.

Shawl will now have 5 shawl sts and 9 edge sts.

Timber Cardigan

by SHANNON COOK

This just might be your new favourite everyday cardigan – it's warm, cozy and versatile. Knitted from the top down, with an easy raglan shaping, Timber is a relaxing knit featuring simple but effective design details. This casual cardigan – designed to be worn open – features twisted ribbing, slimming lines and handy pockets, for a sweater that's as functional as it is beautiful, whether you're at the coffee shop or in the woodshed.

YARN

Brooklyn Tweed Shelter (100% Wyoming-grown Targhee-Columbia Wool, 140yds/128m per 1.76oz/50g skein), shown in Hayloft, worsted

Refer to the **Finished Measurements & Yarn Requirements Chart** on **Page 94** to determine number of skeins required.

GAUGE

16 sts and 26.5 rows = 4in/10cm in St st
16 sts and 26.5 rounds = 4in/10cm in St st, in the round

NEEDLES

5mm/US 8 circular needle, 32in
5mm/US 8 dpns or long circular needle

Adjust needle size if necessary to obtain the proper gauge.

NOTIONS

Removable marker
Stitch markers – 18
Stitch holder
Waste yarn
Yarn needle

STITCH GUIDE

m1L (make one left): With left needle tip, lift strand between needles from front to back. Knit lifted loop through the back. This will make a left-slanting increase.

m1R (make one right): With left needle tip, lift strand between needles from back to front. Knit lifted loop through the front. This will make a right-slanting increase.

SSK (slip, slip, knit): Slip the next 2 stitches, individually, as if to knit, onto the right needle. Insert left needle into the front loops of the slipped stitches and knit them together (through the back loops). This makes a left-slanting decrease.

Twisted Rib Stitch: On right side of work, knit into the back of all knit stitches and work all purl stitches as normal. On wrong side of work, purl into the back of all purl stitches and work all knit stitches as normal.

PATTERN NOTES

This cardigan is intended to be worn with approximately 2in/5cm of positive ease throughout the body and approximately 1.5in/4cm–2in/5cm for the sleeves based on your size chosen.

The cardigan is designed to be worn open. The right and left sides of the cardigan do not come together to meet at the centre of the body. Please choose your size accordingly. The cardigan is knit from the top down, starting with the collar; then the body is worked flat and the sleeves are worked in the round.

Slip all stitch markers as you come to them throughout the pattern.

HOW TO USE THIS PATTERN

1. *Choose your size.* Refer to the **Finished Measurements & Yarn Requirements Chart** on **Page 94**. Select your size based on the **Bust Size** measurements found at the top of the chart. If you prefer a looser or tighter fit, choose a different size, using the **Finished Measurements** to guide you (*sample is shown in Size 34*).

2. *Find your size.* Refer to the **Pattern Chart** on **Page 93**. Mark or highlight the column that contains the information for the size you have chosen.

3. *Fill in the blanks.* Copy the numbers from the **Pattern Chart** on **Page 93** into the blank spaces that correspond to the letters written in the pattern.

NOTE: Measurements are listed in inches and centimetres; larger spaces are provided for these numbers so that you may also include the unit of measurement within that space.

COLLAR

Using the **Ribbed Long Tail Cast-On** (*see* **Stitch Guide** *on* **Page 118**) CO **(A)** _____ sts.

Row 1 (WS): Sl1p wyif, *k1, p1tbl; rep from * to end.

Row 2 (RS): Sl1p wyib, *p1, k1tbl; rep from * to end.

Place removable marker to indicate **RS**.

Rep **Rows 1 & 2** until collar measures 4.25in/10.75cm from CO edge, ending with a **WS** row.

YOKE

RAGLAN INCREASES

Row 1 (Set-Up Row) (RS): Sl1p wyib, p1, [k1tbl, p1] five times, pm, m1R, pm, k1, pm, m1L, pm, [p1, k1tbl] **(B)** _____ times, p1, pm, m1R, pm, k1, pm, m1L, pm, [p1, k1tbl] four times, pm, k9, pm, [k1tbl, p1] four times, pm, m1R, pm, k1, pm, m1L, pm, [p1, k1tbl] **(B)** _____ times, p1, pm, m1R, pm, k1, pm, m1L, pm, [p1, k1tbl] six times. 8 sts inc'd.

Row 2: Sl1p wyif, [k1, p1tbl] five times, k1, sm, p to m, sm, p1, sm, p to m, sm, [k1, p1tbl] **(B)** _____ times, k1, sm, p to m, sm, p1, sm, p to m, sm, [k1, p1tbl] four times, sm, p9, sm, [p1tbl, k1] four times, sm, p to m, sm, p1, sm, p to m, sm, [k1, p1tbl] **(B)** _____ times, k1, sm, p to m, sm, p1, sm, p to m, sm, [k1, p1tbl] six times.

Row 3 (Inc Row): Sl1p wyib, p1, [k1tbl, p1] five times, sm, k to m, m1R, sm, k1, sm, m1L, k to m, sm, [p1, k1tbl] **(B)** _____ times, p1, sm, k to m, m1R, sm, k1, sm, m1L, k to m, sm, [p1, k1tbl] four times, sm, k9, sm, [k1tbl, p1] four times, sm, k to m, m1R, sm, k1, sm, m1L, k to m, sm, [p1, k1tbl] **(B)** _____ times, p1, sm, k to m, m1R, sm, k1, sm, m1L, k to m, sm, [p1, k1tbl] six times. 8 sts inc'd.

Rep **Rows 2 & 3 (C)** _____ times more, ending on a **RS** row.

(D) _____ sts each front (includes 1 raglan st), **(E)** _____ sts each sleeve, **(F)** _____ back sts (includes 2 raglan sts); **(G)** _____ total yoke sts.

RAGLAN INCREASES – FRONT & BACK ONLY

NOTE: Your total sleeve stitch count has now been reached. You will now continue increasing for only the body portion of your cardigan.

SIZE 30

Continue to the **All Sizes – Work Even** section below.

SIZES 32–50

Next Row (WS): Rep **Row 2.**

Next Row (Inc Row): Sl1p wyib, p1, [k1tbl, p1] five times, sm, k to m, m1R, sm, k1, sm, k to m, sm, [p1, k1tbl] **(B)** _____ times, p1, sm, k to m, sm, k1, sm, m1L, k to m, sm, [p1, k1tbl] four times, sm, k9, sm, [k1tbl, p1] four times, sm, k to m, m1R, sm, k1, sm, k to m, sm, [p1, k1tbl] **(B)** _____ times, p1, sm, k to m, sm, k1, sm, m1L, k to m, sm, [p1, k1tbl] six times. 4 sts inc'd.

Rep the last 2 rows **(H)** _____ time(s) more, ending on a **RS** row.

(I) _____ sts each front (includes 1 raglan st) and **(J)** _____ back sts (includes 2 raglan sts); **(K)** _____ total yoke sts.

ALL SIZES – WORK EVEN

Next Row (WS): Rep **Row 2.**

Next Row: Sl1p wyib, p1, [k1tbl, p1] five times, sm, k to m, sm, k1, sm, k to m, sm, [p1, k1tbl] **(B)** _____ times, p1, sm, k to m, sm, k1, sm, k to m, sm, [p1, k1tbl] four times, sm, k9, sm, [k1tbl, p1] four times, sm, k to m, sm, k1, sm, k to m, sm, [p1, k1tbl] **(B)** _____ times, p1, sm, k to m, sm, k1, sm, k to m, sm, [p1, k1tbl] six times.

BODY

Next Row (WS): Sl1p wyif, [k1, p1tbl] five times, k1, sm, p to m, sm, [k1, p1tbl] four times, sm, p9, sm, [p1tbl, k1] four times, sm, p to m, sm, [k1, p1tbl] six times.

Next Row: Sl1p wyib, p1, [k1tbl, p1] five times, sm, k to m, sm, [p1, k1tbl] four times, sm, k9, sm, [k1tbl, p1] four times, sm, k to m, sm, [p1, k1tbl] six times.

Rep the last 2 rows, working even in pattern, until body measures **(O)** _____ from CO sts at underarm, ending with a **WS** row.

Next Row (RS): Sl1p wyib, p1, [k1tbl, p1] five times, sm, m1L, k to m, sm, [p1, k1tbl] four times, sm, k9, sm, [k1tbl, p1] four times, sm, k to m, m1R, sm, [p1, k1tbl] six times. 2 sts inc'd.

Next Row (WS): Sl1p wyif, [k1, p1tbl] five times, k1, **rm**, p to m, **rm**, [k1, p1tbl] four times, **rm**, p9, **rm**, [p1tbl, k1] four times, **rm**, p to 2 sts before m, **rm**, [k1, p1tbl] six times.

You will now have **(P)** _____ total body sts.

POCKET INSERTION

Next Row (RS): Sl1p wyib, p1, [k1tbl, p1] six times, CO **(Q)** _____ sts using **Backwards Loop Cast-On** (*see* **Stitch Guide** *on* **Page 118**), place **(Q)** _____ sts on waste yarn or holder, *k1tbl, p1; rep from * until **(R)** _____ sts left, **k1tbl**, CO **(Q)** _____ sts using **Backwards Loop Cast-On** (*see* **Stitch Guide** *on* **Page 118**), place **(Q)** _____ sts on waste yarn or holder, [p1, k1tbl] seven times.

Next Row: Sl1p wyif, *k1, p1tbl; rep from * to end.

Next Row: Sl1p wyib, *p1, k1tbl; rep from * to end.

Rep the last 2 rows until body measures **(S)** _____ from CO sts at underarm, ending with a **WS** row.

BO in pattern.

SLEEVES

Place **(E)** _____ sts onto long circ or dpns. Rejoin yarn, pick up and knit **(M)** _____ sts along CO edge of underarm, placing a marker (to denote beg of rnd) at centre of picked-up sts so you have an equal number of sts on either side of your existing stitch markers. Join.

(T) _____ total sleeve sts.

Rep the last 2 rows, working even in pattern, until yoke measures **(L)** _____ from base of collar at back neck, ending with a **WS** row.

SLEEVE SEPARATION

Next Row (RS): Sl1p wyib, p1, [k1tbl, p1] five times, sm, k to m, rm, k1, rm, CO **(M)** _____ sts using **Backwards Loop Cast-On** (*see* **Stitch Guide** *on* **Page 118**), place **(E)** _____ sleeve sts (keeping markers in place) onto waste yarn, rm, k1, rm, k to m, sm, [p1, k1tbl] four times, sm, k9, sm, [k1tbl, p1] four times, sm, k to m, rm, k1, rm, CO **(M)** _____ sts using **Backwards Loop Cast-On** (*see* **Stitch Guide** *on* **Page 118**), place **(E)** _____ sleeve sts (keeping markers in place) onto waste yarn, rm, k1, rm, k to m, sm, [p1, k1tbl] six times.

You will now have **(N)** _____ total body sts.

Next Rnd: Knit to m, sm, [p1, k1tbl] **(B)** _____ times, p1, sm, k to end of rnd.

Work even in pattern as established for 1.5in/4cm.

Next Rnd (Dec Rnd): K1, k2tog, k to m, sm, [p1, k1tbl] **(B)** _____ times, p1, sm, k to last 3 sts of rnd, ssk, k1. 2 sts dec'd.

Work **Dec Rnd** every **(U)** _____ until **(V)** _____ sleeve sts remain.

Continue working even in pattern until sleeve measures **(W)** _____ from CO sts at underarm.

CUFFS

SIZES 32, 34, 40, 44 & 46

Next Rnd (Cuff Set-Up): K2tog, p1, *k1tbl, p1; rep from * to end of rnd (remove markers as you come to them). (1 st dec'd)

You will now have **(X)** _____ total sleeve sts.

SIZES 30, 36, 38, 42, 48 & 50

Next Rnd (Cuff Set-Up): *K1tbl, p1; rep from * to 2 sts before end of rnd, p2tog (remove markers as you come to them). 1 st dec'd.

You will now have **(X)** _____ total sleeve sts.

ALL SIZES

Next Rnd: *K1tbl, p1; rep from * to end of rnd.

Rep the last rnd until cuff measures **(Y)** _____ or desired length. BO in pattern.

POCKETS

Place pocket sts from holder back onto needle, rejoin yarn.

Next Row (Pocket Set-Up): K2, m1L, k to last 2 sts, m1R, k2. 2 sts inc'd.

Work even in St st until pocket measures **(Z)** _____.

BO. Do not seam pockets yet – we recommend seaming your pockets after blocking.

FINISHING

Weave in ends and close holes as necessary at underarms. Block garment according to **Finished Measurements** and **Pattern Schematic** shown on **Pages 94** & **95**. Blocking wires can be useful along the two front edges of the cardigan in order to create a nice straight open edge.

After blocking, seam pockets on inside of garment using this recommended method:

http://cocoknits.com/resources/tutorials/sewing-down-pocket-linings/

PATTERN CHART

TO FIT BUST	in	30	32	34	36	38	40	42	44	46	48	50
	cm	76	81.5	86.5	91.5	96.5	102	107	112	117	122	127
COLLAR												
A	Cast-On Collar Stitches	67	67	67	67	67	67	71	71	71	71	71
YOKE												
B	Number of Repeats	3	3	3	3	3	3	4	4	4	4	4
C	Repeats to Work	12	12	13	14	14	15	16	16	17	19	19
D	Front Stitches (including 1 raglan stitch)	27	27	28	29	29	30	31	31	32	34	34
E	Sleeve Stitches (including 0 raglan stitches)	35	35	37	39	39	41	45	45	47	51	51
F	Back Stitches (including 2 raglan stitches)	55	55	57	59	59	61	63	63	65	69	69
G	Total Stitches on Needles	179	179	187	195	195	203	215	215	223	239	239
H	Repeats to Work	0	0	1	2	3	4	5	6	7	7	8
I	Front Stitches (including 1 raglan stitch)	27	28	30	32	33	35	37	38	40	42	43
J	Back Stitches (including 2 raglan stitches)	55	57	61	65	67	71	75	77	81	85	87
K	Total Stitches on Needles	179	183	195	207	211	223	239	243	255	271	275
L	Yoke Length (from base of back collar) in	6.5in	6.75in	7in	7.25in	7.5in	7.75in	7.75in	8.25in	8.25in	9in	9.25in
	cm	16.5cm	17.25cm	17.75cm	18.5cm	19cm	19.75cm	19.75cm	21cm	21cm	22.75cm	23.5cm
SLEEVE SEPARATION												
M	Underarm Stitches	10	12	12	12	14	14	14	16	16	16	18
N	Total Body Stitches	129	137	145	153	161	169	177	185	193	201	209
BODY												
O	Body Length (from underarm to pocket) in	9in	9.5in	10in	10.5in	11in	11.5in	12in	12.5in	13in	13.5in	14in
	cm	22.75cm	24.25cm	25.5cm	26.75cm	28cm	29.25cm	30.5cm	31.75cm	33cm	34.25cm	35.5cm
P	Total Body Stitches	131	139	147	155	163	171	179	187	195	203	211
POCKET INSERTION												
Q	Cast-On Pocket Stitches/Stitches Placed on Holder	14	14	14	14	14	14	16	16	16	16	16
R	Stitches Left in Row	29	29	29	29	29	29	31	31	31	31	31
S	Body Length (from underarm) in	15in	15.5in	16in	16.5in	17in	17.5in	18.5in	19in	19.5in	20in	20.5in
	cm	38cm	39.25cm	40.75cm	42cm	43.25cm	44.5cm	47cm	48.25cm	49.5cm	50.75cm	52cm
SLEEVES												
T	Total Sleeve Stitches	45	47	49	51	53	55	59	61	63	67	69
U	Decrease Round Interval in	1.25in	1.25in	1in	1in	1in	1in	1in	1in	0.75in	0.75in	0.75in
	cm	3.25cm	3.25cm	2.5cm	2.5cm	2.5cm	2.5cm	2.5cm	2.5cm	2cm	2cm	2cm
V	Total Sleeve Stitches	29	31	31	33	33	35	39	41	41	43	43
W	Sleeve Length (from underarm to before cuff) in	11.5in	11.5in	12in	12in	12in	12in	12in	12in	12in	12in	12in
	cm	29.25cm	29.25cm	30.5cm	30.5cm	30.5cm	30.5cm	30.5cm	30.5cm	30.5cm	30.5cm	30.5cm
X	Total Sleeve Stitches	28	30	30	32	32	34	38	40	40	42	42
Y	Cuff Length in	6in	6in	6in	6in	6in	6in	7in	7in	7in	7in	7in
	cm	15.25cm	15.25cm	15.25cm	15.25cm	15.25cm	15.25cm	17.75cm	17.75cm	17.75cm	17.75cm	17.75cm
POCKET												
Z	Pocket Length in	5in	5in	5in	5in	5in	5in	5.5in	5.5in	5.5in	5.5in	5.5in
	cm	12.75cm	12.75cm	12.75cm	12.75cm	12.75cm	12.75cm	14cm	14cm	14cm	14cm	14cm

FINISHED MEASUREMENTS & YARN REQUIREMENTS

BUST SIZE	in	30	32	34	36	38	40	42	44	46	48	50
	cm	76	81.5	86.5	91.5	96.5	102	106.5	112	117	122	127
YARN REQUIREMENTS												
Number of 50g skeins (140yds/128m)		6	6	6	7	7	8	8	9	9	10	11
Metres Required		654	706	764	818	874	931	1022	1090	1146	1235	1302
Yards Required		715	771	835	894	955	1018	1117	1191	1253	1350	1423
FINISHED MEASUREMENTS (in)												
A	Bust/Hip Circumference	32.25	34.25	36.25	38.25	40.25	42.25	44.25	46.25	48.25	50.25	52.25
B	Total Body Length	21.5	22.25	23	23.75	24.5	25.25	26.25	27.25	27.75	29	29.75
C	Body Length (from underarm)	15	15.5	16	16.5	17	17.5	18.5	19	19.5	20	20.5
D	Yoke Length (from base of back collar)	6.5	6.75	7	7.25	7.5	7.75	7.75	8.25	8.25	9	9.25
E	Back Width (mid-underarm to mid-underarm)	16.25	17.25	18.25	19.25	20.25	21.25	22.25	23.25	24.25	25.25	26.25
F	Collar Height	4.25	4.25	4.25	4.25	4.25	4.25	4.25	4.25	4.25	4.25	4.25
G	Border Length	6	6	6	6	6	6	6.5	6.5	6.5	6.5	6.5
H	Arm Circumference	11.25	11.75	12.25	12.75	13.25	13.75	14.75	15.25	15.75	16.75	17.25
I	Sleeve Length (from underarm)	17.5	17.5	18	18	18	18	19	19	19	19	19
J	Cuff Length	6	6	6	6	6	6	7	7	7	7	7
K	Wrist Circumference	7	7.5	7.5	8	8	8.5	9.5	10	10	10.5	10.5
FINISHED MEASUREMENTS (CM)												
A	Bust/Hip Circumference	82	87	92	97.25	102.25	107.25	112.5	117.5	122.5	127.75	132.75
B	Total Body Length	54.5	56.5	58.5	60.25	62.25	64.25	66.75	69.25	70.5	73.75	75.5
C	Body Length (from underarm)	38	39.25	40.75	42	43.25	44.5	47	48.5	49.5	50.75	52
D	Yoke Length (from base of back collar)	16.5	17.25	17.75	18.5	19	19.75	19.75	21	21	22.75	23.5
E	Back Width (mid-underarm to mid-underarm)	41.25	43.75	46.25	49	51.5	54	56.5	59	61.5	64.25	66.75
F	Collar Height	10.75	10.75	10.75	10.75	10.75	10.75	10.75	10.75	10.75	10.75	10.75
G	Border Length	15.25	15.25	15.25	15.25	15.25	15.25	16.5	16.5	16.5	16.5	16.5
H	Arm Circumference	28.5	29.75	31	32.5	33.75	35	37.5	38.75	40	42.5	43.75
I	Sleeve Length (from underarm)	44.5	44.5	45.75	45.75	45.75	45.75	48.25	48.25	48.25	48.25	48.25
J	Cuff Length	15.25	15.25	15.25	15.25	15.25	15.25	17.75	17.75	17.75	17.75	17.75
K	Wrist Circumference	17.75	19	19	20.25	20.25	21.5	24.25	25.5	25.5	26.75	26.75

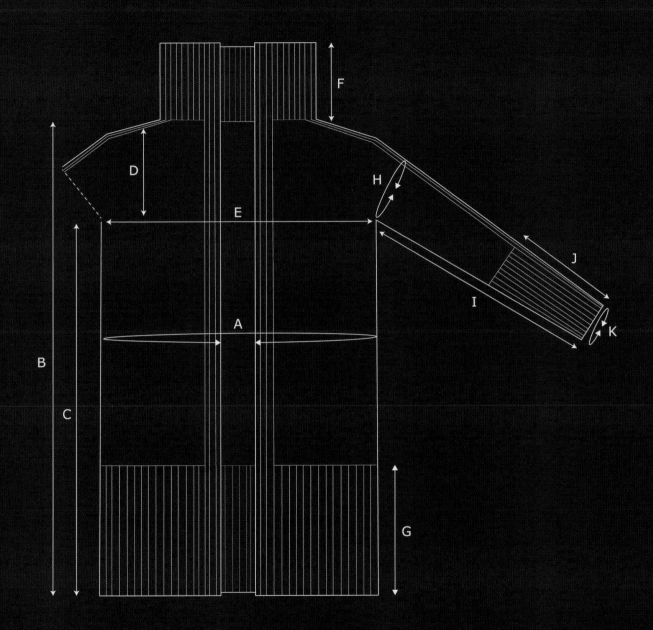

Entwine Scarf

by JANE RICHMOND

Super bulky yarn and big knitting needles make this a fast, fun project for knitters of all skill levels. A fringe made of plump strands of luscious yarn gives the scarf a modern edge. Wind its generous length around once, twice, even three times – or just loop it once and then tie a casual knot. Either way, it's just the thing for a walk in the woods.

YARN

2 skeins Cascade Yarns Magnum (100% Peruvian Highland Wool, 123yds/112m per 8.82oz/250g skein), shown in Colour 9564 OR approx 210yds/191m of super bulky yarn

GAUGE

7.5 sts and 10 rows = 4in/10cm in St st
8 sts and 10 rows = 4in/10cm in pattern

NEEDLES

12mm/US 17 needles

Adjust needle size if necessary to obtain proper gauge.

NOTIONS

Crochet hook (optional)

FINISHED MEASUREMENTS

Approx 88in/2.25m long (with tassels) and 6.5in/16.5cm wide

by JANE RICHMOND

SCARF

Using **Long Tail Cast-On** method, CO 18 sts (*see* **Special Techniques** *on* **Page 120** *for visual tutorial*).

Row 1 (WS): Sl1p, [p2, k2, p1, k2] twice, p3.

Row 2 (RS): Sl1k, [k2, p2, wyib sl1p, p2] twice, k3.

Rep **Rows 1 & 2** until scarf measures approx 74in/1.88m from CO edge, ending with a **RS** row.

BO in pattern.

TASSELS

Step 1: Cut 32 pieces of yarn 16in/40.5cm long.

Step 2: Hold 2 strands together and fold them in half. With wrong side of work facing, use a knitting needle or crochet hook to pull the centre of the folded strands through CO/BO edge to form a loop.

Step 3: Pull all 4 ends of the 2 strands through the loop and cinch tight.

Step 4: Space 8 tassels evenly along each CO/BO edge.

FINISHING

Due to the weight of the recommended yarn and the length of the scarf, I prefer not to block this accessory.

If you feel it necessary, I recommend a light steam blocking rather than wet blocking, as the plumpness of the slipped stitch columns tends to be lost if the fabric gets stretched out or weighed down after soaking.

Tread Hat

by SHANNON COOK

Twisted Rib and Garter stitches combine in this cozy, textured topper. In super soft merino with a luxe faux fur pom pom, this hat will take you from a morning at the farmers' market to an evening by the campfire without a backward glance. With three sizes and a wide range of yarns to choose from (it looks just as good in regular worsted as it does in chainette), you just might find yourself making multiples.

YARN

1 skein Woolfolk FAR (100% Merino, 142yds/130m per skein, chainette), shown in Colour #1 OR approx 142yds/130m of worsted weight chainette yarn

GAUGE

16 sts and 25 rows = 4in/10cm in St st on larger needles, in the round

NEEDLES

5mm/US 8 (for ribbing)
16in circular needle OR 32in circular needle for Magic Loop Method
6mm/US 10 (for body of hat)
16in circular needle and dpns OR 32in circular needle for Magic Loop Method

Adjust needle size if necessary to obtain proper gauge.

NOTIONS

Stitch marker
Yarn needle
Bernat Faux Fur Pom Pom in colourway Grey Linx

SIZING

Adult Small (Adult Medium and Adult Large) to fit head circumference 21 (22, 23)in/53 (56, 58)cm

FINISHED MEASUREMENTS

Approx 17 (18, 19)in/43 (46, 48)cm brim circumference (unstretched) and 9.25 (9.25, 9.75)in/23.5 (23.5, 25)cm height, blocked

PATTERN NOTES

If making a pom pom (in place of faux fur pom pom) for your hat, you may require additional yarn.

If substituting regular worsted weight yarn (in place of chainette yarn), you may need additional or slightly less yarn than indicated above.

DIRECTIONS | tread hat

by SHANNON COOK

RIBBING

Using the **Long Tail Cast-On** and smaller needles, CO 70 (80, 90) sts (*see* **Special Techniques** *on* **Page 120** *for visual tutorial*).

If using a 32in circ for the **Magic Loop Method**, pm at end of cast-on sts to denote start of round. Join in round, distributing stitches evenly onto both needles, being careful not to twist (*see* **Stitch Guide** *on* **Page 118** *for link to visual tutorial*).

If using a 16in circ, pm at end of cast-on stitches to denote start of round. Join in round, being careful not to twist.

Rnd 1: *[K1tbl, p1] three times, [k1, p1] twice; rep from * to end of rnd.

Rep **Rnd 1** until ribbing measures approx 2in/5cm from CO edge (or until desired length).

BODY

Switch to larger needles.

Rnd 1: *[K1tbl, p1] twice, k1tbl, p5; rep from * to end of rnd.

Rnd 2: *[K1tbl, p1] twice, k1tbl, k5; rep from * to end of rnd.

Rnds 3–6: Rep **Rnds 1 & 2** twice.

Rnds 7 & 8: Rep **Rnd 2** twice.

Rnds 9–32: Rep **Rnds 1–8** three times more.

NOTE: If you would like to add more slouch to your hat, repeat **Rows 1–8** *once more.*

SIZES SMALL AND MEDIUM

Rnd 33: Rep **Rnd 1**.

Hat should now measure approx 7.5in/19cm from CO edge.

SIZE LARGE

Rnds 33 & 34: Rep **Rnds 1 & 2**.

Rnd 35: Rep **Rnd 1**.

Hat should now measure approx 8in/20cm from CO edge.

CROWN

If using a 16in circ, change to dpns as you work the first decrease round.

ALL SIZES

Rnd 1: *[K1tbl, p1] twice, k1tbl, k2tog, k1, k2tog; rep from * to end of rnd. 14 (16, 18) sts dec'd. 56 (64, 72) sts

Rnd 2: *[K1tbl, p1] twice, k1tbl, p3; rep from * to end of rnd.

Rnd 3: *[K1tbl, p1] twice, k1tbl, k2tog, k1; rep from * to end of rnd. 7 (8, 9) sts dec'd. 49 (56, 63) sts

Rnd 4: *[K1tbl, p1] twice, k1tbl, p2; rep from * to end of rnd.

Rnd 5: *[K1tbl, p1] twice, k1tbl, k2tog; rep from * to end of rnd. 7 (8, 9) sts dec'd. 42 (48, 54) sts

Rnd 6: *[K1tbl, p1]; rep from * to end of rnd.

Rnd 7: K2tog to end of rnd. 21 (24, 27) sts dec'd. 21 (24, 27) sts

Rnd 8: K1tbl to end of rnd.

Rnd 9: *K2tog, k1; rep from * to end of rnd. 7 (8, 9) sts dec'd. 14 (16, 18) sts

Rnd 10: K2tog to end of rnd. 7 (8, 9) sts dec'd. 7 (8, 9) sts

Hat should now measure approx 9 (9, 9.5)in/23 (23, 24)cm from CO edge.

Cut yarn, leaving a 6in/15cm tail. Use yarn needle to thread end through remaining sts. Pull tight and tie off.

Weave in ends and wet block your hat to finished measurements. Attach a pom pom if desired for extra flair!

NOTE: If using a faux fur pom pom (as shown on sample) attach securely in multiple places at top of crown.

Woolfolk is a soft yarn, so the pom pom needs to be attached in several places in order for hat not to sag in back.

Woodstack Mittens

by JANE RICHMOND

Textured mittens stitched in plump worsted weight yarn create pillows of warmth for cold hands – just the thing for brisk fall nights and cold winter days. With an easy-to-memorize grid stitch pattern and basic shaping, these mittens knit up quickly, making them a weekend project when you need a new set of winter accessories. And since the pattern is available in three different sizes, they're a great gift knit, too.

YARN

1 ball Patons Classic Wool Worsted (100% Pure New Wool, 210yds/192m per 3.5oz/100g ball), shown in Natural Mix 00229 OR 158yds/144m of worsted weight yarn

GAUGE

17.5 sts and 24 rows = 4in/10cm in St st on larger needles
19.25 sts and 28 rows = 4in/10cm in pattern on larger needles

NEEDLES

4mm/US 6 dpns or long circular needle for Magic Loop Method
4.5mm/US 7 dpns or long circular needle for Magic Loop Method

Adjust needle size if necessary to obtain proper gauge.

NOTIONS

Stitch markers – 3
Waste yarn
Yarn needle

SIZE

Adult Small (Adult Medium, Adult Large)

FINISHED MEASUREMENTS

Approx 7 (7.5, 8)in/18 (19, 20.5)cm hand length (not including cuff) and 7 (8, 8.75)in/18 (20.5, 22)cm hand circumference (unstretched)

STITCH GUIDE

Kitchener Stitch
For helpful instructions, see **Stitch Guide** on **Page 118**.

CUFF

Using **Long Tail Cast-On** and smaller needles, CO 32 (36, 40) sts (*see* **Special Techniques** *on* **Page 120** *for visual tutorial*).

Divide sts evenly among 3 needles if working on dpns. PM and join for working in the rnd, being careful not to twist.

Rnd 1 (1 x 1 Ribbing): [K1, p1] to end of rnd.

Rep **Rnd 1** until cuff measures 3in/7.5cm.

HAND

SHAPE THUMB GUSSET

Change to larger needles.

Rnd 1 (Set-Up): Kfb, k14 (16, 18), pm, [kfb] twice, pm, k14 (16, 18), kfb. 36 (40, 44) sts.

Rnd 2: Kfb, purl to last st, kfb. 38 (42, 46) sts.

Rnd 3: P1, [k1, p1] to marker, sm, kfb, [k1, p1] to one st before marker, kfb, sm, k1, [p1, k1] to end of rnd. 40 (44, 48) sts.

Rnd 4: [P1, k1] to end of rnd.

Rnd 5: Knit to marker, sm, kfb, knit to one st before marker, kfb, sm, knit to end of rnd. 42 (46, 50) sts.

Rnd 6: Purl.

Rep **Rnds 3–6** until there are 12 (14, 16) sts between two thumb markers, ending with **Rnd 6 (4, 6)**. 46 (52, 58) sts.

WORK EVEN

Beg with **Rnd 1 (3, 1)**, work the following four rnds until hand measures 2.25 (2.5, 2.75)in/5 (6.5, 7)cm from top of ribbing at wrist, ending with **Rnd 2**.

Rnds 1 & 2: [P1, k1] to end of rnd.

Rnd 3: Knit.

Rnd 4: Purl.

Next Rnd (Separate Thumb from Hand): Knit to marker, rm, place 12 (14, 16) thumb sts onto waste yarn, rm, join to continue working in the rnd, knit to end of rnd. 34 (38, 42) sts.

Rnd 1: Purl.

Rnds 2 & 3: [P1, k1] to end of rnd.

Rnd 4: Knit.

Rep **Rnds 1–4** until hand measures approx 5.75 (6.25, 6.75)in/14.5 (16, 17.5)cm from ribbing, ending with **Rnd 3**.

MITTEN TOP SHAPING

Rnd 1: [Skp, k13 (15, 17), k2tog] twice. 30 (34, 38) sts.

Rnd 2: Purl.

Rnd 3: P2tog, [k1, p1] 5 (6, 7) times, k1, p2tog, skp, [p1, k1] 5 (6, 7) times, p1, k2tog. 26 (30, 34) sts.

Rnd 4: [P1, k1] to end of rnd.

Rnd 5: [Skp, k9 (11, 13), k2tog] twice. 22 (26, 30) sts.

Rnd 6: Purl.

Rnd 7: P2tog, [k1, p1] 3 (4, 5) times, k1, p2tog, skp, [p1, k1], 3 (4, 5) times, p1, k2tog. 18 (22, 26) sts.

Rnd 8: [P1, k1] to end of rnd.

Break yarn, leaving a 30in/76cm tail, use **Kitchener Stitch** (*see* **Stitch Guide** *on* **Page 118**) to graft top of hand closed.

THUMB

Remove waste yarn and return 12 (14, 16) thumb sts to needles. With **RS** facing, rejoin yarn at crook of thumb, leaving a long enough tail to close the gap that appears where thumb meets hand. Distribute sts evenly among your needles and join for working in the round.

Rnd 1: Knit.

Rnd 2: Purl.

Rnds 3 & 4: [K1, p1] to end of rnd.

Rep **Rnds 1–4** until thumb measures 2in/5cm from top of thumb gusset (where thumb meets hand), ending with **Rnd 4**.

Next Rnd: [K2tog] 6 (7, 8) times.

Break yarn and thread through remaining 7 sts, pull tight and tie off to secure. Weave in ends. Use the tail of the rejoined yarn to close any holes left where thumb meets hand.

Fireside Pullover

by JANE RICHMOND

This classic pullover is knit top down, in the round, in quick-to-work bulky yarn. Begin with the shapely shawl collar and then pick up stitches for the yoke; ribbing hugs the upper body for a flattering fit over the shoulders and upper arms. Subtle waist and hip shaping gives the garment a feminine silhouette; the deep ribbed cuffs and hem up the cozy factor. You'll reach for this sweater again and again on late nights and lazy Sunday mornings.

YARN

Cascade Yarns Ecological Wool (100% Undyed Peruvian Highland Wool, 478yds/437m per 8.75oz/250g skein), shown in Beige (8016), bulky

Refer to the **Finished Measurements & Yarn Requirements Chart** on **Page 116** to determine number of skeins required.

NOTIONS

Stitch markers – 4

Waste yarn

Yarn needle

Large buttons – 1 or 2 (optional)

GAUGE

17 sts and 21.5 rows = 4in/10cm in St st on larger needles, in the round

NEEDLES

5.5mm/US 9 circular needle, 32in (*for collar and body*)

5.5mm/US 9 dpns or long circular needle for Magic Loop Method (*for sleeves*)

5mm/US 8 circular needle, 32in (*for hem*)

5mm/US 8 dpns or long circular needle for Magic Loop Method (*for cuffs*)

Adjust needle size if necessary to obtain proper gauge.

STITCH GUIDE

Wrap & Turn: Slip the next stitch purl-wise, bring the yarn to the front (or back on purl rows), return the slipped stitch to the LH needle and bring the yarn to the back (or front on purl rows); turn the work and continue as directed. Knit or purl into the wrap as well as the stitch when you reach these wrapped stitches on subsequent rows.

m1L (make one left): With left needle tip, lift strand between needles from front to back. Knit lifted loop through the back. This will make a left-slanting increase.

m1R (make one right): With left needle tip, lift strand between needles from back to front. Knit lifted loop through the front. This will make a right-slanting increase.

SSK (slip, slip, knit): Slip the next 2 stitches, individually, as if to knit, onto the right needle. Insert left needle into the front loops of the slipped stitches and knit them together (through the back loops). This makes a left-slanting decrease.

PATTERN NOTES

If substituting yarn, it is recommended to choose a wool or wool blend to provide rigidity and stability to the collar and fabric of the garment.

Sizes 34 and 48 each use the full number of skeins required. This does not include yarn for swatching.

HOW TO USE THIS PATTERN

1. Choose your size. Refer to the **Finished Measurements & Yarn Requirements Chart** on **Page 116**. Select your size based on the **Bust Size** measurements found at the top of the chart. If you prefer a looser or tighter fit, choose a different size, using the **Finished Measurements** listed to guide you (*model is shown wearing Size 34 with 2in/5cm of negative ease*).

2. Find your size. Refer to the **Pattern Chart** on **Page 115**. Mark or highlight the column that contains the information for the size you have chosen.

3. Fill in the blanks. Copy the numbers from the **Pattern Chart** on **Page 115** into the blank spaces that correspond to the letters written in the pattern.

NOTE: Measurements are listed in inches and centimetres; larger spaces are provided for these numbers so that you may also include the unit of measurement within that space.

COLLAR

Using **Turkish Cast-On** and larger circ, CO 36 sts (*see **Special Techniques** on **Page 121** for visual tutorial*).

FIRST HALF / RIGHT SIDE

Work in **1 x 1 Ribbing** until collar measures 4in/10cm from **Turkish Cast-On**. For a nice clean edge, slip the first stitch of every row of collar until yoke is joined for working in the rnd.

Row 1 (Short Row): [K1, p1] across first 32 sts, W&T, [k1, p1] to end of row.

Row 2 (Short Row): [K1, p1] across first 28 sts, W&T, [k1, p1] to end of row.

Row 3 (Short Row): [K1, p1] across first 24 sts, W&T, [k1, p1] to end of row.

Row 4 (Short Row): [K1, p1] across first 20 sts, W&T, [k1, p1] to end of row.

Row 5 (Short Row): [K1, p1] across first 16 sts, W&T, [k1, p1] to end of row.

Row 6 (Short Row): [K1, p1] across first 12 sts, W&T, [k1, p1] to end of row.

Row 7 (Short Row): [K1, p1] across first 8 sts, W&T, [k1, p1] to end of row.

Row 8 (Short Row): [K1, p1] across first 4 sts, W&T, [k1, p1] to end of row.

Row 9: [K1, p1] to end of row, picking up wraps as you come to them on the 5th, 9th, 13th, 17th, 21st, 25th, 29th, and 33rd sts.

Rows 10–12: [K1, p1] to end of row.

Row 13 (Short Row): [K1, p1] across first 4 sts, W&T, [k1, p1] to end of row.

Row 14 (Short Row): [K1, p1] across first 8 sts, picking up wrap on 5th st as you come to it, W&T, [k1, p1] to end of row.

Row 15 (Short Row): [K1, p1] across first 12 sts, picking up wrap on 9th st as you come to it, W&T, [k1, p1] to end of row.

Row 16 (Short Row): [K1, p1] across first 16 sts, picking up wrap on 13th st as you come to it, W&T, [k1, p1] to end of row.

Row 17 (Short Row): [K1, p1] across first 20 sts, picking up wrap on 17th st as you come to it, W&T, [k1, p1] to end of row.

Row 18 (Short Row): [K1, p1] across first 24 sts, picking up wrap on 21st st as you come to it, W&T, [k1, p1] to end of row.

Row 19 (Short Row): [K1, p1] across first 28 sts, picking up wrap on 25th st as you come to it, W&T, [k1, p1] to end of row.

Row 20 (Short Row): [K1, p1] across first 32 sts, picking up wrap on 29th st as you come to it, W&T, [k1, p1] to end of row.

Row 21: [K1, p1] to end of row, picking up wrap on 33rd st as you come to it.

Row 22 (Dec Row / Begin on Short Edge): Ssk, [k1, p1] to end of row. 1 st dec'd.

Row 23 (Dec Row / Begin on Long Edge): [K1, p1] to last 3 sts, k1, p2tog. 1 st dec'd.

Rep **Rows 22 & 23** five times more. 24 sts.

SECOND HALF / LEFT SIDE

Break yarn and place sts from first half of collar onto st holder or waste yarn. Reattach yarn to tail end of **Turkish Cast-On**. The first st is a slip knot; drop it off the end of the needle and pull to undo. 36 sts.

Row 1: [K1, p1] to end of row.

Work **First Half / Right Side** of collar once more.

*NOTE: Short-row shaping rows always begin on the Outside Edge (Long Edge) of the collar (see **Pattern Schematic** on **Page 117**).*

YOKE

Row 1 (Set-Up Raglan Shaping): PM, with working yarn and RH needle pick up and knit **(A)** _____ sts evenly along *Inside Edge (Short Edge)* of collar as follows: **(B)** _____ left sleeve sts along curved section of collar, pm, **(C)** _____ back neck sts along straight section of collar, pm, **(B)** _____ right sleeve sts on curved section of collar, pm, place live sts of **First Half / Right Side** of collar onto a dpn and work across in rib [k1, p1] to end of row. **(D)** _____ sts.

Row 2 (WS): [K1, p1] to end of row.

Row 3 (Raglan Inc Row)(RS): *[K1, p1] to marker, m1R, sm, k1, m1L, p1, rep from * three times more, [k1, p1] to end of row. 8 sts inc'd.

Row 4: *[K1, p1] to last st before marker, p1, sm, p1, rep from * three times more, [k1, p1] to end of row.

Row 5 (Raglan Inc Row): *[K1, p1], to last st before marker, k1, m1R, sm, k1, m1L, rep from * three times more, [k1, p1] to end of row. 8 sts inc'd.

Rep **Rows 2–5** until there are **(E)** _____ front sts (each side), **(F)** _____ sleeve sts (each sleeve), and **(G)** _____ back sts; **(H)** _____ total yoke sts. End with **Row 2**.

Work even in **1 x 1 Ribbing** until yoke measures **(I)** _____ from picked up edge at back neck, ending with a **WS** row.

Next Row (RS): [K1, p1] to last marker, sm, knit to last **(J)** _____ sts of row, slip these last sts onto a dpn or spare circ.

BODY

Next Rnd:
Join for working in the rnd as follows: Hold **(J)** _____ slipped sts on spare needle in front of the first **(J)** _____ sts on LH needle, so that the right front collar overlaps the left. Knit these overlapping sts together (one st from spare needle with one st from LH needle) to complete the collar and join the yoke for working in the rnd.

Continue Rnd:
Separate sleeves from body as follows: *Knit to marker, rm, place **(F)** _____ sleeve sts onto waste yarn, rm, using **Backwards Loop Cast-On** (*see* **Stitch Guide** *on* **Page 118**), CO **(K)** _____ sts placing a marker at the centre of these cast-on sts; rep from * once more, knit across to centre of overlapped sts and pm to denote beg of rnd.

(L) _____ total body sts.

Work even in St st, until body of pullover measures 4in/10cm from CO sts at underarm.

WAIST SHAPING

Next Rnd (Dec Rnd): *Knit to 3 sts before marker, ssk, k1, sm, k1, k2tog, rep from * once more, knit to end of rnd. 4 sts dec'd.

Work even for 3in/7.5cm, rep **Dec Rnd** once more.

(M) _____ total body sts.

Work even until pullover measures **(N)** _____ from picked-up edge at back neck.

HIP SHAPING

Next Rnd (Inc Rnd): *Knit to 1 st before marker, m1R, k1, sm, k1, m1L, rep from * once more, knit to end of rnd. 4 sts inc'd.

Work even, repeating **Inc Rnd** every 1.5in/4cm three times more.

(O) _____ total body sts. Pullover should measure **(P)** _____ from picked-up edge at back neck.

Change to smaller circ and work in **1 x 1 Ribbing** for 3in/7.5cm. Beginning the ribbing at the left underarm will make the transition less noticeable. BO in rib.

SLEEVES

Place **(F)** _____ sleeve sts onto larger dpns or long circ. Rejoin yarn, pick up and knit **(K)** _____ sts along CO edge of underarm, placing a marker at centre of cast-on stitches to denote beg of rnd. Join.

(Q) _____ total sleeve sts.

Work even in St st until sleeve measures 1in/2.5cm from CO sts at underarm.

Next Rnd (Dec Rnd): K1, k2tog, knit to last 3 sts of rnd, ssk, k1. 2 sts dec'd.

Work **Dec Rnd** every **(R)** _____ until **(S)** _____ sleeve sts remain.

Work even until sleeve measures **(T)** _____ from CO sts at underarm.

Change to smaller needles and work in **1 x 1 Ribbing** for 3in/7.5cm. BO in rib.

FINISHING

Weave in ends and block garment according to **Pattern Schematic** shown on **Page 117**. Add button closure if you would like the option to wear the collar buttoned up. For helpful visual instructions, we like the following tutorial:

http://ysolda.com/support/tutorials/sewn-button-loops/

TO FIT BUST		in	28	30	32	34	36	38	40	42	44	46	48
		cm	71	76	81.5	86.5	91.5	96.5	101.5	106.5	112	117	122
YOKE													
A	Pick Up Along Collar		42	42	42	42	42	34	36	36	48	40	40
B	Sleeve Stitches		8	8	8	8	8	4	4	4	8	4	4
C	Back Neck		26	26	26	26	26	26	28	28	32	32	32
D	Total Yoke Stitches		90	90	90	90	90	82	84	84	96	88	88
E	Front Stitches (each side)		36	38	40	42	42	44	46	46	46	48	50
F	Sleeve Stitches (each sleeve)		32	36	40	44	44	44	48	48	52	52	56
G	Back Stitches		50	54	58	62	62	66	72	72	76	80	84
H	Total Yoke Stitches		186	202	218	234	234	242	260	260	272	280	296
I	Raglan Depth	in	6.25in	6.5in	6.75in	7in	7.25in	7.5in	8.25in	8.5in	8.75in	9in	9.75in
		cm	16cm	16.5cm	17cm	18cm	18.5cm	19cm	21cm	21.5cm	22cm	23cm	25cm
J	Overlapped Stitches of Collar		22	22	22	22	22	22	20	20	16	16	16
BODY													
K	Cast-On at Underarm		6	8	8	8	12	12	12	14	14	16	16
L	Total Body Stitches (bust)		112	124	132	140	148	156	168	172	180	192	200
M	Total Body Stitches (waist)		104	116	124	132	140	148	160	164	172	184	192
N	Work Even	in	16.25in	16.5in	16.75in	17in	17.25in	17.25in	17.5in	17.5in	17.75in	17.75in	18in
		cm	41.5cm	42cm	42.5cm	43cm	44cm	44cm	44.5cm	44.5cm	45cm	45cm	45.5cm
O	Total Body Stitches (full hip)		120	132	140	148	156	164	176	180	188	200	208
P	Body Length	in	21.25in	21.5in	21.75in	22in	22.25in	22.25in	22.5in	22.5in	22.75in	22.75in	23in
		cm	54cm	54.5cm	55cm	56cm	56.5cm	56.5cm	57cm	57cm	58cm	58cm	58.5cm
SLEEVES													
Q	Total Sleeve Stitches		38	44	48	52	56	56	60	62	66	68	72
R	Decrease Round Interval	in	–	3.5in	3in	2in	1.75in	1.75in	1.75in	1.5in	1.5in	1.25in	1.25in
		cm	–	9cm	7.5cm	5cm	4.5cm	4.5cm	4.5cm	4cm	4cm	3cm	3cm
S	Total Wrist Stitches		36	36	38	38	40	40	44	44	46	46	48
T	Sleeve Length (to underarm)	in	15.5in	15.5in	16in	16in	16in	16in	16.5in	16.5in	16.5in	16.5in	17in
		cm	39.5cm	39.5cm	40.5cm	40.5cm	40.5cm	40.5cm	42cm	42cm	42cm	42cm	43cm

FINISHED MEASUREMENTS & YARN REQUIREMENTS

BUST SIZE		in	28	30	32	34	36	38	40	42	44	46	48
		cm	71	76	81.5	86.5	91.5	96.5	101.5	106.5	112	117	122
YARN REQUIREMENTS													
Number of 250g skeins (478yds/437m)			2	2	2	2	3	3	3	3	3	3	3
Metres Required (includes partial skeins)			676	756	818	874	931	960	1041	1068	1127	1183	1254
Yards Required (includes partial skeins)			740	827	895	956	1018	1050	1139	1168	1233	1294	1372
FINISHED MEASUREMENTS (IN)													
A	Bust		26.25	29.25	31	33	34.75	36.75	39.5	40.5	42.25	45.25	47
B	Waist		24.5	27.25	29.25	31	33	34.75	37.75	38.5	40.5	43.25	45.25
C	Hip		28.25	31	33	34.75	36.75	38.5	41.5	42.25	44.25	47	49
D	Body Length (from base of back collar)		24.25	24.5	24.75	25	25.25	25.25	25.5	25.5	25.75	25.75	26
E	Raglan Depth		6.25	6.5	6.75	7	7.25	7.5	8.25	8.5	8.75	9	9.75
F	Hem to Underarm		18	18	18	18	18	17.75	17.25	17	17	16.75	16.25
G	Arm Circumference		9	10.25	11.25	12.25	13.25	13.25	14	14.5	15.5	16	17
H	Sleeve Length (from underarm)		18.5	18.5	19	19	19	19	19.5	19.5	19.5	19.5	20
I	Back Neck		6	6	6	6	6	6	6.5	6.5	7.5	7.5	7.5
J	Wrist		8.5	8.5	9	9	9.5	9.5	10.25	10.25	10.75	10.75	11.25
FINISHED MEASUREMENTS (CM)													
A	Bust		67	74	79	83.5	88.5	93	100.5	103	107.5	114.5	119.5
B	Waist		62	69.5	74	79	83.5	88.5	95.5	98	103	110	114.5
C	Hip		71.5	79	83.5	88.5	93	98	105	107.5	112.5	119.5	124.5
D	Body Length (from base of back collar)		61.5	62	63	63.5	64	64	65	65	65.5	65.5	66
E	Raglan Depth		16	16.5	17	18	18.5	19	21	21.5	22	23	25
F	Hem to Underarm		45.5	45.5	46	45.5	45.5	45	44	43.5	43.5	42.5	41
G	Arm Circumference		22.5	26.5	28.5	31	33.5	33.5	36	37	39.5	40.5	43
H	Sleeve Length (from underarm)		39.5	39.5	40.5	40.5	40.5	40.5	42	42	42	42	43
I	Back Neck		15	15	15	15	15	15	16.5	16.5	19	19	19
J	Wrist		21.5	21.5	22.5	22.5	24	24	26.5	26.5	27.5	27.5	28.5

PATTERN SCHEMATIC

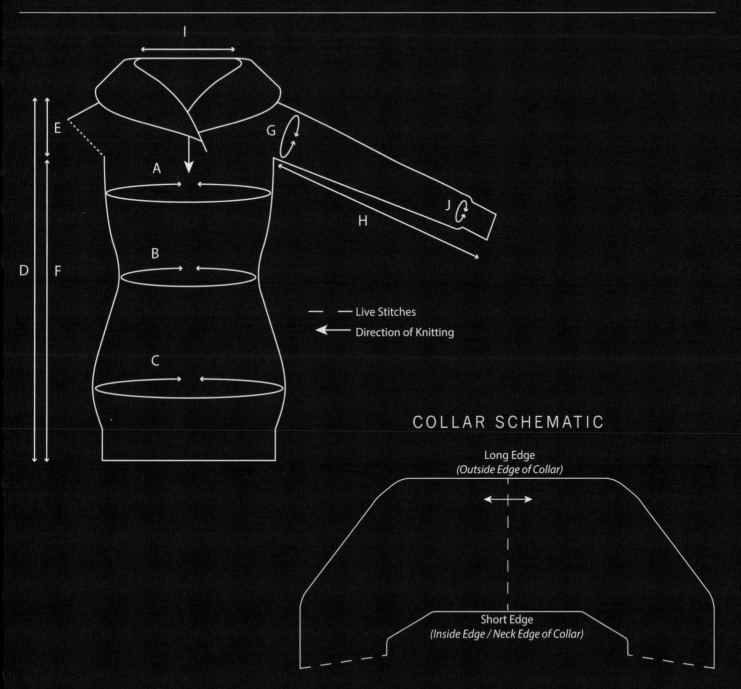

I

E

A

G

D F

B

H

J

C

— — Live Stitches

⟵ Direction of Knitting

COLLAR SCHEMATIC

Long Edge
(Outside Edge of Collar)

Short Edge
(Inside Edge / Neck Edge of Collar)

CAST-ON METHODS

Backwards Loop Cast-On (during knitting): With stitches on your right needle, wrap working yarn around your left index finger from back to front. Insert tip of right needle under front of loop on finger. Remove finger and pull yarn gently to snug loop around needle. Take care not to make your loops too tight or too loose.

Cable Cast-On: For helpful visual instructions, we like the following:
http://www.knittinghelp.com/video/play/cable-cast-on-english

Long Tail Cast-On: For visual tutorial see **Page 120**.

Ribbed Long Tail Cast-On: For helpful visual instructions, we like the following: *http://www.knittingdaily.com/blogs/knitting-daily/cast-on-with-eunny/*

Turkish Cast-On: For visual tutorial see **Page 121**.

INCREASES

m1 (EZ's Backwards Loop Version): With stitches on your right needle, wrap working yarn around your left index finger from back to front. Insert tip of right needle under front of loop on finger. Remove finger and pull yarn gently to snug loop around needle. On next row treat the loop as a separate stitch. Take care to pull the stitch nice and tight so it blends in.

m1L (make one left): With left needle tip, lift strand between needles from front to back. Knit lifted loop through the back. This will make a left-slanting increase.

m1R (make one right): With left needle tip, lift strand between needles from back to front. Knit lifted loop through the front. This will make a right-slanting increase.

DECREASES

SSK (slip, slip, knit): Slip the next two stitches, individually, as if to knit, onto the right needle. Insert left needle into the front loops of the slipped stitches and knit them together (through the back loops). This makes a left-slanting decrease.

METHODS

Magic Loop Method: For helpful visual instructions, we like the following: *http://www.marianraepublications.com/tutorials*

SHORT ROW SHAPING

Wrap & Turn: Slip the next stitch purl-wise, bring the yarn to the front (or back on purl rows), return the slipped stitch to the left needle and bring the yarn to the back (or front on purl rows). Turn the work and continue as directed. Knit or purl into the wrap as well as the stitch when you reach these wrapped stitches on subsequent rows.

STITCHES

Openwork Stitch:

Row 1 (RS): Knit.
Row 2: Purl.
Rows 3, 4 & 6: Knit.
Row 5: *K2tog, yo; rep from * to end.

Twisted Rib Stitch: On right side of work, knit into the back of all knit stitches and work all purl stitches as normal. On wrong side of work, purl into the back of all purl stitches and work all knit stitches as normal.

FINISHING

Kitchener Stitch: Break yarn, leaving a 30in/76cm tail. If using dpns, divide front and back stitches evenly onto two needles. If using Magic Loop Method, stitches should already be divided appropriately.

Step One: With RS facing, insert needle through first stitch on front needle as if to purl.

Step Two: Insert needle through first stitch on back needle as if to knit.

Step Three: Insert needle through first stitch on front needle as if to knit; drop this stitch from needle. Insert needle through next stitch on front needle as if to purl.

Step Four: Insert needle through first stitch on back needle as if to purl; drop this stitch from needle. Insert needle through next stitch on back needle as if to knit.

Repeat **Steps Three & Four** until two stitches remain (one on front needle and one on back). Insert needle through stitch on front needle as if to knit; drop this stitch from the needle. Insert needle through stitch on back needle as if to purl; drop this stitch from the needle.

Abbreviations

approx	approximately
beg	beginning
BO	bind-off
CC	contrast colour
circ	circular needle
CO	cast-on
dec('d)	decrease(d)
dpn(s)	double pointed needles
inc('d)	increase(d)
k	knit
kfb	knit through front and back
k1tbl	knit one stitch through the back loop
k2tog	knit two stitches together
k3tog	knit three stitches together
LH	left hand
MC	main colour
m1	make one stitch
m1L	make one left (*see* **Stitch Guide** *on* **Page 118**)
m1R	make one right (*see* **Stitch Guide** *on* **Page 118**)
p	purl
pm	place marker
p1tbl	purl one stitch through the back loop
p2tog	purl two stitches together
rep	repeat
RH	right hand
rm	remove marker
rnd(s)	round(s)
RS	right side
skp	slip one, knit one, pass slipped stitch over
sl	slip
sl1k	slip one stitch knit-wise
sl1p	slip one stitch purl-wise
sm	slip marker
ssk	slip, slip, knit (*see* **Stitch Guide** *on* **Page 118**)
st(s)	stitch(es)
St st	Stockinette stitch
WS	wrong side
W&T	wrap and turn (*see* **Stitch Guide** *on* **Page 118**)
wyib	with yarn held in back
wyif	with yarn held in front
yo	yarn over

Special Techniques

LONG TAIL CAST-ON

long tail

ball of yarn

Step One: Make a slip knot with a long tail—use approximately 1in/2.5cm of yarn per cast-on stitch needed. Hold needle with your right hand, and with yarn hanging down, separate the two pieces with your index finger and thumb so that the ball end of the yarn is around your index finger and the long tail is around your left thumb.

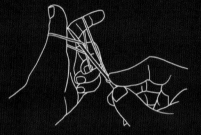

Step Two: Bring needle down in front of thumb and insert tip under the loop that is wrapped around your thumb.

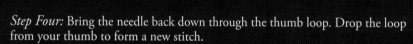

Step Three: Bring the tip of needle over the yarn in front of the index finger and enter the loop wrapped around that finger from above.

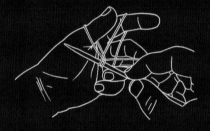

Step Four: Bring the needle back down through the thumb loop. Drop the loop from your thumb to form a new stitch.

Step Five: Separate the yarn with your index finger and thumb again as in Step One; snug the stitch up if it is too loose. Repeat Steps One–Five until the desired number of stitches is reached.

Follow the Arrow: Up the thumb, down the finger, through the middle of the thumb loop, then release the thumb loop.

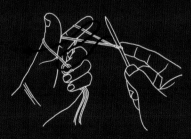

Special Techniques

TURKISH CAST-ON

This provisional cast-on method creates a subtle faux seam down the centre of the collar of the **Fireside Pullover** (see **Page 108**). It yields a tidy, flat "seam" with identical right and wrong sides. As an alternative, you may wish to use Judy's Magic Cast-On, which produces a slightly more "seamless" right side and a noticeable faux seam on the wrong side of the collar.

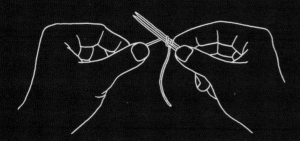

For the Turkish Cast-On, you will need one long circular needle, two shorter circular needles, or two double pointed needles.

Step One: Holding the needle tips parallel to each other with your right hand, and with tips facing the same direction, place a slip knot on the top needle and begin wrapping the yarn around both needles.

Step Two: Without counting the slip knot, make 36 wraps.

Step Three: Turn the needles 180 degrees so that the top needle with the slip knot is now on the bottom. Hold with your left hand, and with your right pull the bottom needle so that the wraps are sitting on the cable.

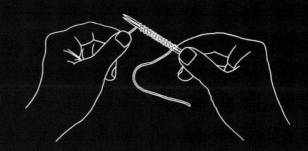

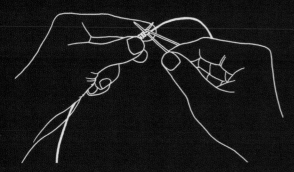

Step Four: Using a double pointed needle, work across stitches of top needle in k1, p1 ribbing.

Step Five: Turn your work. Using a second double pointed needle, work in rib across the same stitches from Step Four.

Continue as instructed on **Page 110**, by working these same stitches (first half of collar) with two double pointed needles and leaving the provisional cast-on on the circular needle to be worked later. You could also transfer the cast-on stitches to a stitch holder if you prefer.

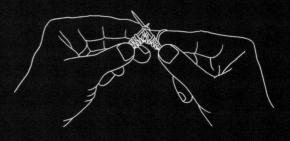

Sources

BROOKLYN TWEED

info@brooklyntweed.com
www.brooklyntweed.com

CASCADE YARNS

425.970.4644
www.cascadeyarns.com

PATONS

inquire@yarnspirations.com
www.patonsyarns.com

WOOLFOLK

info@woolfolkyarn.com
www.woolfolkyarn.com

Thank Yous

We would like to thank the following people for their invaluable support throughout the making of *Within*....

Anne Marie Hart for her tireless work tech editing our patterns. She truly has a magical eye and that special touch.

Kelsey Goodwin for bringing our "story" to life with her photography. We can't wait until the next one!

Our testers – thank you all so very much for your endless hours of knitting, helpful feedback, support, and friendship. You play such a special and important role in this process.

Austen Gilliland for making sure we don't need to call the grammar police. And to *Jessie Kwak* and *Lisa Fielding*, for making sure things are "just right."

Our models, *Gryffin Hoskins* and *Mark Spencer* – thank you for your patience and endurance, and for braving the cold to help bring our book to life. You guys are the best.

To our knitter friends – we adore you. Without you we would not be making our dreams become reality. We thank you for your continued support and friendship, and for making such a wonderfully warm community a joy to be a part of.

JANE

To my sweet Elsie, who is always so patient and understanding when Mom needs a few extra minutes after hours to get work done! You are my motivation and inspiration, my love.

To my family for their continued love and support while I chase my dreams and take the road less travelled.

To all of my friends, near and far, new and old, in the flesh and online, knitters and non-knitters, you lift me up and you support me unconditionally, and for that I am truly grateful.

To each and every knitter who has ever supported me and my work – whether it be through the purchase of patterns or books, recommending them to a friend, suggesting my video tutorials, reading my blog, following me on social media, or even just a kind word in my inbox! I couldn't have done any of this without each and every one of you – thank you from the bottom of my heart for your continued support.

And to Shannon – for always being there and never wavering. You are the most driven perfectionist in everything you do – you set the bar.

SHANNON

Thank you from the bottom of my heart to my wonderful and patient husband for being my best friend and constant sounding board, for making me laugh, and for always being there for me – I love you.

To my two beautiful daughters, who inspire me daily, and always encourage and motivate me to continue to reach for my dreams. I love you both to the moon and back.

To my parents and grandparents, who raised me with a love and respect for the beauty of the handmade and the written word. I'm so blessed to have such a loving and supportive family who are my constant cheerleaders.

To all of my wonderful friends (both online and in person), who have filled my days with laughter, friendship, and kindness, I thank you for always being there. And to the amazing knitting and sewing community – you guys truly allow me to live out my dreams each day! Thank you for continuing to support my passions, for reading all these years, and for making. You all inspire me so much, and I thank you for your continued friendship and support.

And to Jane – thank you for being there for me. I'm so happy to call you my friend (and biz partner) and it has been a joy to watch you on your own path of self-discovery throughout the making of *Within*. Bloom, my love, the sun is shining on you.

78

86

96

100

104

108

127

About The Authors

JANE RICHMOND

Jane Richmond is a knitwear designer, author, and publisher, living on Vancouver Island. She has been self-publishing her designs since 2008; she blogs about the process – and her inspiration – at www.janerichmond.com.

Known for her classic aesthetic and clearly written patterns, Jane delivers designs that are fun to knit and easy to wear, with an appealing casual style.

Jane is the author and co-publisher of *Island* (Marian Rae Publications, 2012), and the co-author and co-publisher of *Seasonless* (Marian Rae Publications, 2014), and *Journey* (Marian Rae Publications, 2013). Her work has also appeared in *Cascadia: Knits from the West Coast* (Cooperative Press, 2013) and *November Knits: Inspired Designs for Changing Seasons* (Interweave Press, 2012).

WWW.JANERICHMOND.COM

SHANNON COOK

Shannon Cook is a knitting and sewing pattern designer, author and publisher, and the writer behind the popular blog www.veryshannon.com. She is happily living a handmade life near the ocean on Vancouver Island with her husband and two daughters.

Shannon designs patterns for the modern knitter. With their engaging textures, vibrant colours, and striking lines, her fun, dynamic garments and accessories are destined to become wardrobe staples.

Shannon is the co-author and co-publisher of *Sesaonless* (Marian Rae Publications, 2014) and *Journey* (Marian Rae Publications, 2013), and co-publisher of *Island* (Marian Rae Publications, 2012). Her work has also appeared in *3 Skeins or Less – Modern Baby Knits* (Interweave, 2016) and *Fat Quarters: Small Fabrics, More than 50 Big Ideas* (Lark Crafts, 2015).

WWW.VERYSHANNON.COM

DON'T MISS OUR OTHER TITLES

ISLAND: A COLLECTION

By Jane Richmond

A collection of five handknits designed by Jane Richmond and inspired by life on Vancouver Island.

ISBN-10: 0991728904
ISBN-13: 978-0-9917289-0-9

JOURNEY: A COLLABORATION

By Jane Richmond & Shannon Cook

A collaboration of six handknits from designers Jane Richmond and Shannon Cook, inspired by the journey of self-discovery, independence, and the path back to yourself.

ISBN-10: 0991728912
ISBN-13: 978-0-9917289-1-6

SEASONLESS: MINI COLLECTION, VOLUME 1

By Jane Richmond & Shannon Cook

Styles change and trends change, but the seasons of life stay the same. Stable. Trustworthy. Ever dependable. Just like your favourite knits.

Seasonless is mini collection of three handknits from Jane Richmond and Shannon Cook. The pieces are designed to be versatile, wearable, and effortless – the kind of knitwear that never has a place in your closet because you are always wearing it.

WWW.MARIANRAEPUBLICATIONS.COM